About This Thing Called Love

Jennifer Scarborough

BookLeaf Publishing

India | USA | UK

Presentation by *BookLeaf Publishing*

Web: www.bookleafpub.com

E-mail: info@bookleafpub.com

ISBN: 978-93-5744-919-9

First edition 2022

DEDICATION

To My Muse, My Him, My Inspiration-

In this endeavor I desire to share with you the longings of my heart, the capacity of my mind and the depths of my soul. If ever I fall short in my expression of admiration for you, Husain A. Gatlin please read these words and be reminded that you are LOVED

The Moment

The yearning for another
Feeling complete but not yet whole
As if someone was holding captive
The very Essence of my soul
Desire fueled a burning passion
That brightly boisterous flame
That flickers at the sight of you
Or the mention of your name
And yet my shyness keeps me hidden
From making you aware
For our love it is forbidden
Though I wish that you were near
So I'll reconcile with longing for now
With loneliness I make atonement
Until we are as one someday
I'll wait patiently for our moment

The Reason

If this is true, if this is deep
And you shall remain mine to keep
Love will be the reason

Full of love, no need to lust
You have my honor and my trust
Truth will be the reason

If truth should mean that growth may sting
As we face the challenges life may bring
Growth will be the reason

As we grow old and seasons change
As what was once familiar now seems strange
Change will be the reason

As the winds of change bring love anew
Forever will I belong to you
Love will be the reason

The Question

Ask me anything you'd like and I'll tell the truth
Sometimes my humanness will hurt you
And I am living proof
 That I suck at being loved
 But I'm great at loving others
 If I'm afraid I run or fight
And I'm not saying that makes it right
But I'll be back one way or another
And I want you to understand me
Even though I don't let you in
A walking contradiction you say
Damn where do I begin
To tell the man that I love that I can't
Even sleep without him at night
But the fear of vulnerability won't let me say
That I need you here with me
So I pretend to be ok whether you stay or if you
leave

What am I doing?!

The Answer

You saw through the core of me
The love, the pain
The sun, the rain
The day, the light
The dark, the night
The joy, the grief
The chaos, the peace
The ebb, the flow
The dull, the glow
The in, the out
The silence, the clout
The near, the far
The wound, the scar
And became the answer that led me where I was
meant to be

The Friendship

Tell me that you'll love me when you don't like
me
And if we should ever end
You'll remain without a doubt, the best version
of a friend
And when I say those things to hurt you
That you'll find compassion to forgive
And that when I feel like dying
You'll inspire me to live
And when things get hard and life is not fine
Maybe we'd feel better if we parted
That you still see a best friend in me and
remember why we started

The Fight

I'm angry, I'm livid
I'm too loud, or too timid
Too sexy, too much
Or am I just not enough
I'm confused, feel misused
Damn, So much frustration
We've Become enemies
Lack of communication
I'm mad, I'm pissed
I'm talking shit
I can't do this anymore
I've said horrible things
Need a drink at the bar
You deserved every word
Did I take it too far?

The Break Up

I call the girls to discuss the madness
They sense the sorrow and the sadness
And a broken heart it feels like dying
Can't utter a word, can't stop crying
I pick up my things, I return the keys
Pride has brought lovers down to their knees
Maybe I wasn't wrong, neither were you
But we choose this for us, now what do we do?

The Forgiveness

I'm sorry can't fix what I've done
So I write you a letter
To make it all better
And pray that forgiveness soon comes
I've lashed out in anger
Said my goodbyes
Without giving the whys
You must feel like your loving a stranger
So I wait by the phone
Just hoping you'll call
Damn we've been through it all
I'm on the edge I'm in danger
And I pray we make peace
And our love doesn't cease
And I pray that forgiveness soon comes

The Silence

PLEASE HOLD ME
When we've exhausted verbal resources
And created language barriers
With mixed emotions
And made mountains of non verbal
Communication so treacherous
we dare not attempt to climb them
PLEASE HOLD ME
When all the shame and hurt drown us
As the weight of pride shackles our feet
And we can't swim to safety
And the life raft of love seems just beyond reach
PLEASE HOLD ME
when the sadness in our eyes
Displays the pain in our hearts
And the silence says all
That which we cannot
PLEASE HOLD ME

The Prayer

I manifested this man, this love
This unbound energy
I sat before the altar and begged the universe
That you'd appear in this life for me
To have and hold, to love and grow
To be sure of something, without doubt to know
That you were mine even before
this life,
That I'd be your partner, your best friend, your
wife
I prayed to fulfill your deepest needs
And give life to Legacy as you sowed the seed
Of love unbound by time or space
In my dreams, I'd see your face
And know that if we were meant to be
That you'd find your way back to me

The Journey

At times it seems, this love is biblical
Heaven sent and then it's cyclical
To hell we go and back again
In the flesh and metaphysical
Torn And tattered
Bruised and Battered
Like some sadistic love/hate ritual
Repeated Pattern
Hearts all shattered
The con job is neuro chemical
Some love sick shit
That I just don't get
Do you think I'm fucking expendable
Behavior is beyond reprehensible
And just when I think I'm broken
I'm bendable
Although we've been to the brink,it's mendable
AndI'm willing to go all the way to the end with
you

The JOURNEY

The Rest

Lay on my chest
Listen to the rhythm
As my heart beats for you
And we breathe in tandem
Becoming one with our bodies
And unified in our sin
Sharing energy through touch
As I seep into your skin
And you trace the outside of my body
I give you my best
You lay here inside me and I give you rest

The Peace

Comfort, compassion
Love everlasting
We find a solution
Conflict resolution
No holding grudges
she bends and he budges
It's not always a dream
But we're always a team
This is how we found PEACE

The Lesson

I brought you fear and you gave me trust
We knew it was love, they all thought it was lust
You brought me Ego and I gave you soul
We both arrived broken, we both left here whole
I brought you sadness and you helped me cope
We both came here defeated, we left here with
hope
You brought me gifts and I gave you art
We both had difficult endings that gave us a new
start
And throughout our love, we learned such a
valuable lesson
That even what appears at first as the worse,
often leads to the blessing

The Promise

At the touch of your skin,
My heart will race
I give you my all, my breath, my space
I see love when I see your face
I see heaven deep in your eyes
Within your soul mine also lies
For you have been my saving grace
This I Promise

The Surrender

My ego has arrived at your door,
Bruised and bloody and wanting no more
Broken, she's Waving her flag of defeat
She falls to the floor and kneels at your feet
She put up a battle, one hell of a fight
She's kept me from harm all
The days of my life
Made sure that no matter how trials beat me
down
That she'd always be there if no one was around
And I've learned to be grateful for all
Her protection
After each disappointment, betrayal or rejection
She endured every hardship and past every test
But she now deserved peace, and much needed
rest
And I no longer needed my ego alive
Because I was not surviving, I knew how to
thrive
So I laid her to slumber, the false self- the
pretender
Farewell my dear Ego, My Love- I surrender

The Redemption

My gift, my curse
My better, my worse
My cause, my cure
My tainted, my pure
My now, my then
My forever again
As love remains constant contradiction
I've found in you, the end of fear
And that is my redemption

About this thing called Love

It feels like…
The birds in the sky
The bees in the flowers
The seconds to minutes
And minutes to hours
The dusk and the dawn
Fresh dew on the lawn
The sway of the trees
in the gentlest breeze
The moon and the stars
Or deep convos in cars
The hows and the whys
The You's And the I's
The me became Us
The building of trust
The wrongs and the rights
The laughter, the fights
The bitterness and the breakups
The passionate make ups
all of the challenges that we've made it through
I'd do it all again, just to do it with you

About this thing called love